T0290099

AM IN BED WITH YOU

EMMA BARNES

I AM IN BED WITH YOU

AUCKLAND
UNIVERSITY
PRESS

For Simon George and my chosen family

Contents

This is a creation myth

This is a creation myth   3

Meat   5

Reading   6

Passive-aggressive letter to a john   7

Standing   8

Mother's Day   9

The Factory   10

I am a man   15

Maiden Mother Crone   17

Ohio   18

I am in bed with you   19

Landslide   23

Sigourney Weaver in your dreams

Sigourney Weaver and the Dream Father   27

Sigourney Weaver and I go to bed   28

Sigourney Weaver buys property in Aro Valley   29

Sigourney Weaver and I rent a movie   30

I take ecstasy with Sigourney Weaver   31

Sigourney Weaver and I come down   32

Sigourney Weaver and I go through Suicide Tuesday together   33

Sigourney Weaver helps me out of some feelings (not pants)   34

Sigourney Weaver and I renegotiate our boundaries   35

Sigourney Weaver and I play video games at Wizards   36

Sigourney Weaver seduces me with the purchase of a van   37

Sigourney Weaver gets citizenship and goes to a ceremony   38

Sigourney Weaver and the impregnation   39

Sigourney Weaver in the womb   40

I birth Sigourney Weaver's android baby   41

Sigourney Weaver confronts the limits of desire   42

Sigourney Weaver and I break up   43

Sigourney Weaver brushes my hair   44

Sigourney Weaver and I correspond only via email   45

Sigourney Weaver becomes the witch of the block   46

The Run-Around

Give up   49

The heel of your palm   50

The cap of my shoulder   51

Hot spit   52

The vermilion line   53

I invite myself inside   54

Low boughs   55

The butter knife   56

To be known   57

Completely dry riverbed   58

Begin again   59

Cut   60

Down   62

You are a horrible goose   63

Before you arrive   64

There is no good ending   65

This is a love poem   66

Emptied   67

Good girl, good girl   68

Previously published works   71

Acknowledgements   72

This is a
creation myth

I am deliberate
and afraid
of nothing.
—Audre Lorde, 'New Year's Day'

This is a creation myth

The woman impregnated the man and his belly swelled full of tadpoles. They lay on collapsible sun chairs eating crackers out of boxes until the children arrived. The first one hurled hula hoops in front of it, rolling and tumbling through them while breathing fire. The second child, as always, had a lot to live up to. That child balanced books on its head and juggled water balloons. Though this feat was equally challenging, the audience felt it was only a four out of five compared to the previous entertainer.

When the third child made its way out of its father's belly, it was just a tadpole. You can't always be what you want to be even if your mother and father are Makers. Or children of Makers. Or even if – well, you get the picture. The man wanted to spew the tadpoles from his mouth in a wave of wiggling water, but the woman said that her people had produced a steady stream of one child after one child after one child for centuries and would it be okay if he just did that because it was what she was used to and she would

feel more comfortable with the whole procreation process if she had a foot in the door in terms of the method of dispersal. For a while there were just children. A belly can hold quite a few. Probably about an hour later a child came out that transformed into a cockerel with a red comb and then into a cat and then into the words 'No comment' written in curls of parmesan cheese on blue cut-pile carpet made of 100% pure New Zealand wool. The audience clapped more from confusion than any other sentiment.

The next four children created a planet through a series of interpretive dances and prodigious vomits. The one who vomited the magma probably had the hardest row to hoe. Although the one who puked up tiny bamboo tree after tiny bamboo tree might have had a strong argument had it not been puking for what was a remarkably long time. That child was understandably tired and sore and not really in the mood for a good debate on the 'who had it worse' front. I think we can all agree that vomiting bamboo or magma wasn't really high on our list of priorities when we woke this morning. The next child presented herbs and such, in an arrangement reminiscent of a bouquet garni but on a more melodramatic scale. No one really knew what to do about this since it didn't seem related to the tasks at hand. 'So, it has come to this,' said the man with a belly slightly less full of tadpoles than it had been at a previous moment in time. The woman leaned forwards and sniffed deeply. Her flaring nostrils lent a certain *je ne sais pour*

quoi to the whole situation. In the middle there was a pause where the earlier children fought with the later children over trivialities. Some spit flew and the man and the woman opened a new box of crackers and discussed the scene. The oldest child split itself open and revealed itself again and again as companies of smaller selves. The youngest shook head to toe spraying children like drops of water over the ranks. Several other children chopped themselves into pieces each one a new tiny tadpole. The yard crowded with bodies.

By the time it grew dark there were too many children to count. They were a huddled mass of fishy tails and acrobatic tricks. Arms shot skyward searching for space and everyone took breath in concert. There were small fights. Several children sustained bites. The man and the woman got up from their sun chairs and took a bow in front of the gathered brood and disappeared in a puff of smoke. This was much like everyone expected. The children picked up their tricks and set off for grandma's.

Meat

I know many women who are growing embryos. I had hoped it was done in mason jars with water by now. But I have been informed that it's still much meatier than that. My mason jar was ready to go. I had a jug of water even. But you know what kids are like these days. I question the wisdom of the process but, of course, most advice is fairly straightforward. In most cases the meat complies freely, maybe you could even say eagerly. I'm not sure I could ask for said meat to do much more than exist. But then, meat just seems to do its thing, with or without my higher meaty functions. The growth of the next generation of meat people seems tenuous when you consider the lumbering vulnerability of a pregnant person, their meat encasing newer meat. The smaller meat person suspended in juices that require the meat incubator to keep on keeping on. It was the expulsion of small meat products that killed pregnant people either in the act or later from wear and tear that leads to meaty decline. Rotting. It is difficult to say meat over and over in the context of humanity. We don't like to consider ourselves chewed up, swallowed and defecated by some higher-rung occupant. It is hard to imagine what is above your meat when the meat focuses as if at an apex. As if at the apex with an unwillingness to remember that our meat is fragile, our bones flimsy, and something else, inevitably, has bigger teeth.

Reading

I learned to read the weather at his knee, at his beck and call. I look into a face to see the headland, the forming clouds. I will call it a storm five days in advance. I interpret the signs inside the signs before the signs are signs. Boxers telegraph their next move. I saw yours last week. I'm waiting for it to arrive. When the punches land I am waiting for the next round. I don't bother to pick up what you're putting down. I live in the future then the past. You are always in the middle speaking to me through layers that are me seeing what I expected to see then looking for the next trick. I don't know how anything makes it inside me. Which may explain why nothing makes it inside me. I hollowed myself out to make room for everything he wanted me to be. And I've filled the space ever since with worry, with the little nightmares that seep into the daytime and with faces. All your faces. They roll up through me, a yearbook of bad decisions. Of missed connections. Of reconsidered invitations. I am outside of time. I am inside myself. I'm never going to hear what you're saying to me.

Passive-aggressive letter
to a john

The same, the story of the same, women who are too similar rarely get on, you're as bad as each other, oh you fight because you're so similar, it can't be helped, I can only apologise, of course it nearly destroyed me, he loves you, I totally and utterly reject your assertions, oh you know there are two people in every relationship, I'm sure it never occurred to you, of course you enable him, girls don't speak in loud voices, you sound like a foghorn, you haven't been pregnant, no one would ever be good enough, just because someone is powerful doesn't mean they aren't also tiny and small, to be fair, did you think about all the things you did wrong, my pain is larger than your pain, you're just so intimidating, perhaps you shouldn't be so serious, just laugh more, everything is a joke, oh she sobbed so terribly, it's an inherently manipulative position, so much unspoken tension, if only you would straighten up and fly right.

Standing

This is a premonition of a conversation about your value and worth that will happen on a Monday with your mother. Only the glossed-over version of the truth for her where no one hurts and she can be simple and happy. We are all perfect in her rear-view mirror. Don't say a word against this dogma. The time for emotional skills is not now. They've made a dress in the shape of the perfect daughter and now they'd like you to put it on. The bonds of affection are tight and they will photograph you against your will. But you've put on clothing before. You've dressed yourself for years. And it slides off your body like it is a paper-doll creation with tabs to hold it on instead of laces or zips or domes. When you've created yourself outside the view of your family they can no longer see you. Their eyes glide over the shapes you made and look into the cracks they put there. They only see the hard wall of you that says no. But underneath there you're a city or a forest or both. You built a galaxy with your fingers and they want you to play Connect Four where they always win because their pain is the loudest to them. You won't resolve this in a week or a day but you are standing again within twenty-four hours.

Mother's Day

I lie down, motherless. I'm a specific form of ache that is the missing of a woman with years on me. I think about her. Could she tell me about how she grew herself into a person. How she found herself in mid-life to lose herself again regularly just for the finding, the coming home. My own mother I undo like laces. My own mother wanted the shape of my body to be understandable. I was on my own with my mind. She was at war with my body. Day to day of years and years alone in my room losing myself to shapes she wouldn't understand, to the cause of invisibility. She was a silence. The background sound in a track where my father controlled me like a marionette. The strings were anger. The dance was never-ending. The duty of family is a heavy coat I took off and put in a cupboard the day that man told me he should never have let me go. It can be hard to find yourself under a layer of acceptable quiet. The mouths of Irish Catholics are stuffed so full of guilt nothing else ever comes out. Anglicans won't say anything at all. The cleanest body is the one that doesn't exist. I made myself as small as possible but I still couldn't stop it existing. That I am here at all is all my work. But there are days, like today, where I imagine a mother. Where I imagine me.

The Factory

1.

When I am a woman I will have long legs like my mother. I will reach the top cupboard with the arms that match the legs. I will be able to see myself in the mirror. When I am a woman my name will sound like an apple. When I am a woman babies will fall from between my legs like seeds, like silt. When I am a woman I will be able to reach the tall door handles in the factory. I won't get shut inside in the cold. Even if I did my voice would be so loud you could hear me in another street, perhaps two. When I am a woman I will wear new clothes. I will only wear blue dresses that fly out in a circle when I spin around. Nothing will touch my neck if I don't want it to, when I am a woman.

2.

The factory is cold. It echoes. It is dark and I can't reach the light switch. I call out but no one hears me. I call out again. I spend time reaching for the door handle. My body should be able to grow like a tree. I should always be taller. In the time that passes my muscles start to ache as if my sides are stretching as if I am growing. But I am not growing. I am panicking. When I am a woman I will not have to panic. I will not panic. The factory smells like milk. Milk. Vanilla. More milk. Cold milk. At least I am not locked in the freezer – no one would hear me there. The doors automatically shut. Creaking. I am too small to stop them.

3.

I fall off my bike. My head wound is a gusher. Bleeding and bleeding and bleeding. I am dressing like the 70s in the 80s but soon I will need a new wardrobe. My mother uses my clothing to staunch the blood. I have a head wound but all I can think is my t-shirts, my t-shirts. When they sew my head closed I can feel it pulling through the skin. My mother has to leave because she will faint. I am there while they stitch and sew and pull. I am again alone when weeks later they take out the stitches. This time the pulling is painful. It is painful but they don't stop. My reward, this muddy scar.

4.

I am in love constantly. You, me. Love around the house. Love when I am in my room. Love riding my bike to school. The heart-racing push. I burn, tamping down above skin. My body awoke as a different person. But I was still there following it around. I was layers. A cake. A fat cake. A cake obsessed with its own inferiority. You, as boys only succeeded in confirmation. You confirmed my inferiority. You confirmed you were teenaged boys. But I was still learning. I was learning the cello and the piano and I sang and I rode my bike back and forth and I started to fill notebooks and I kept up I kept up. In winter in kilts in summer with cotton button-front uniforms. I kept up.

5.

I discover invisibility. A habit. I wear only men's clothes. Cardigans and corduroy. My legs roar as the fabric rubs against itself. I grow my hair long like curtains. I turn my eyes inwards. Invisibility comforts me. I wrap it around myself against the stares. They received eyes as presents for Christmas, I heard. Still it is not enough. I wear steel-toed boots and pretend at aggression. Or rather I pretend that the aggression is pretend. To be looked at. I want to never be looked at. Stop looking at me. Stop seeing this me. I am not this version of me you're seeing but I can't get out.

6.

I am reading. I read her. She reads me inside with tunnels and skin and words. We live in opposite hemispheres. In one hemisphere we gather. I hold each of her breasts in each of my hands. She is looking at me and seeing something else. I look at her and see her Midwestern nose. Her skin white from snow-covered months. The thing she sees in me is half of a murderous pair. She is romantic about the two. I know that a brick in a stocking covered in a mother's blood is not romantic. But I am me. She comes from *O High O*. I come from a southern school of realistic expectations about who can love me. This school teaches gratitude in the face of almost everything. I'm a fast learner.

7.

I roll into. I roll. I am round. If I hide enough. If I hide enough. On the street I am yelled at. If I hide enough they won't notice me. If I say nothing. If I am nothing. I am nothing why can't they already see that. Some of them see that. You see that. Ten times over you see that. Nothing. Nothingness. Nowhere really. Backwards. Still nothing. You see that I'm nothing. You see that I'm nothing. You see. I don't eat anything. I am keen to become nothing faster. One November when you aren't looking, all I think about is the knife drawer. Knives. But you're no longer looking. No one is looking. The gravity of my own body keeps me trapped in a bed. Nothing. The knife drawer is in the kitchen. Too far away.

8.

When I am ten years old a teacher of my parents' acquaintance describes my hips as perfect for child-bearing. I remember this because my mother was incredulous. From ten she was like a skyscraper. Her incredulity made her head wobble. From where I stood it was the sun glinting off her head. When I am nineteen I overhear a father talking with a group of men about young women's breasts. I turn around and walk away. When I am all the ages of woman someone calls me F-A-T. When I am twenty-three a man tells me I am not wife material. I only pay attention to where my body registers something. A pinch, pain. But I keep walking. Someone takes my hand.

9.

When I am a woman it won't matter. When I am a woman I will answer every question asked within the same word. When I am a woman you will stop looking at me like this. When I am a woman from an apple seed I will grow a tree. When I am a woman I will have all my teeth. When I am a woman I will control my body. When I am a woman I will only drink water. When I am a woman I will be so hungry I will eat an island. When I am a woman I will buy milk in ships. When I am a woman I will say.

I am a man

'Here she is' they say of my body.
I lifted my breasts into my clothing this morning.

I say. I am a man for all weathers. A man
for all withers. You said: The horse is loose.

I capital I capital I start these sentences in my
head on the night I have an existential crisis

about my gender. I am a man because I think
I am a man. I am in this body of hips and

that wet cave between my legs. You say your
father is a woman. I say she makes sense. I'm

a woman but no one takes these breasts seriously.
There's only so far I can get in this. Men want me

to be a woman. You want me to be a woman. I am
the praying mantis destroyer of worlds and you can't

explain why you want to be devoured. Acting out
woman in this woman shape is standing on the

ground while people fly around me. I am a bird of
cheeping and plumage. No one said a word about

flying. Is this a telescope of longing? Am I upside
down and my brain transforms the image? It's all

in the bricks. It's me the plasterer, the decorator,
the twin of my twin. I am the grand misogynist

behind the curtain, my cunt a billow of satin lining.
Or I'm just kidding myself sweetly. Where to now

with this wilting self I've kept in a jar? See me as a
woman-man shape. See me as I backflip back into

myself. See me as I disappear when I can't hold the
ideas inside me. Daily, I am a woman climbing default.

Maiden Mother Crone

When I stand my thighs moan like a generation of abandoned children. Descending into the crone straight from maiden I'm no mother except to myself. My skin is a web of folds of rights and wrongs. Time is the flat circle of my breasts. I'm such sweet repetition you'd never know to look at me that I am the same problem repeated. I suffered at the hands of absent fathers and invisible mothers. I mothered myself and ignored the need of a father. What could a man tell me of being myself. I'm a boy and a man and a crone. I used sticks to build my spine and fat to build my shape and I threw iron to the moon to grow musculature. I went into the houses and beds of friends and strangers to learn edges and gaps and games. I spoke in a loud voice, my only voice, just to hear myself think. Draw the curtains, the crone wants to kiss in private. Pour the wine. Bring out the verse. Let me tangle my bony fingers in your long curls so I may draw you in closer just in case I'm going to eat you like the death that waits for you at the end of everything. The crone knows. She tastes you like the air, like the same wine in both our mouths. She cannot know herself. But she knows you. And as she stands her thighs groan like the generation of electricity in a time of drought. We're as dry as her bones. As empty as the next lake bed.

Ohio

We make out awkwardly on the bed.
And her shifting weight is a tide or the back of the bus.

Have you seen her lately?
Not since she moved out.

When we go to a costume party together she
wears a lycra body suit and duct tapes a dildo

to her crotch. It bumps against me in the darkness
like a bottle-nosed dolphin or a chair lift.

Outside the party she kisses me again, her
costume insistent. She has been dead for

two-and-a-half years. She lay down to sleep
at thirty-six and her heart failed. Like it

failed a test or failed a warrant or failed to
come in to work that day like everyone else.

My fingernail split down to the cuticle and
she climbed into my bed at dawn smelling

of chemicals and the last stand of the hospice.
She moved out on my birthday and I ripped

up the note she wrote. I ripped up the note
she left me that she wrote me, when she left.

I am in bed with you

I am in bed with you. The room varies. But I'm always on the
left. I am pulling the pieces of myself into myself. In the winter
I left myself behind in the 90s. I'm coming back now. You
can see the light touching me. I can see layers of tissue finally
making a body. And once I have a body I have a head. And in
my head are these thoughts. I can't tell you what it is like with
words. You can hold my hand and feel my pulse, but I was in
1994. I didn't like

it there. When I am getting through days I don't even know I
am making it. I am the legume in that story about royalty. And
then on the other side I open up like a lake into a river. I can
survey the lean fields of my insides as if I am the owner of all
those glistening blades. In 1994 I was fourteen. I buried some-
thing back there. I buried it alive in a biscuit tin. This winter
makes choices I'd have made differently. Your mother cooked
a roast chicken every

Saturday unless a larger animal had died. You taste chicken
fat, the crackle of dry skin. The kitchen like a church, like a cake,
like a kitchen. *Der Kuchen. Die Küche. Die Kirche.* The German
teacher is Danish. The German teacher is a man with a golf club
handle in his hands. He is buried in that biscuit tin. He's not
alone. The taste of chicken fat. The ache of pubescent breasts.
He dines with the others on the scraps of winter hoardings.
He chews a turnip end and runs through

conjugated verb endings, this time in French. *E, es, e, ons, ez,
ent. Je parle. Tu parles. Il parle. Nous parlons. Vous parlez. Ils parlent.*
He is flaking apart in the seventeen years of my memory failing.
I restart myself with a jumper cable. The cure for my gaps is
voltage. The cure for me is a car battery and a back room. I have

cured myself of myself spring after spring after spring. But
still, here I am with holes the size of holes inside me, tethered
under a Dacron bed cover bought before I was. I've

had my bed made for me. And now I am in it. 1994, when
everyone missed Kurt Cobain except those people who didn't
miss Kurt Cobain. Or didn't know Kurt Cobain. Kurt Cobain
hovered over teenage beds. Kurt Cobain was dead before I
figured out I was alive. I may have been dead before I figured
out I was a person. I may be a corn husk when I grow up. My
career aspirations have always been pedestrian. I make the
darkness when I close my eyes. In there I

find the silence. In there I find my limbs numb, my dumb
brim, my rims glum. You shoot for a high score when you
hand me the pills I will down tonight. No drink for me. Take
me straight to the overall feeling of wellbeing. Take me to the

heavy sleep. I can hold myself up there without the weight
of imagining pain in the bodies of others. And the ruru goes
ruru. And in the dark his mate sounds a kiwi call and the
ruru goes *ruru*. The right T-bars are handmade. They have

a web of leather. They cost four times the pair on my feet.
The German teacher wears heavy leather shoes. One English
teacher tells me her surname means paddock. We write about
her in a made-up language on our books. At some point I

have to start existing in the future. Tomorrow I'll exist in the
future. Tomorrow I'll be forty with a mane of hair and a rowboat
in the garage that we'll take into the harbour and float in. We
make onion dip in hats and eat it. I call you-at-fifteen up on

the phone and you try to make me say 'clitoris' out loud. I
harvest my organs 5th-period Science and watch a rat's liver
glisten. Sometimes the teachers talk quietly and say things we
aren't supposed to hear. Things as yet we are unable to bear.

Reasons to say no hide in the woods like animals and I do not
have the time, nor the inclination to hunt them and land their
bloody carcasses upon the front of my late model ute that
started its life in Japan on a conveyor belt. If you know what

I mean. You should know I say that as a vegetarian. You should
know that this is a story about where I came from. I rode trains
in Japan for hours, alone. Between the middle of the river and
elsewhere a deer was trapped, chest deep in

snow her ears aflutter. I think you know what noise I'm making
here. The panting of a deer trapped in a partly

frozen river. The rhythm of the train sheltered me through
time. Between the serial killer tying women to concrete blocks

and submerging them and the quiet walk back to an empty
apartment. Alone in Japan I waited and waited. And then

like a baby rat I was born again without anyone noticing. In
that darkness and dankness I opened my eyes and wanted to

die. In that dimness I lay flat on my back and went nowhere
for years. My skin a rock ledge. My skin, keratin. The problem

with being an oracle is that the signs only make sense to you.
My brain becomes a viscous fluid for most of the morning. In

this story my mother is a red carton of milk on a desk, consumed

by children. I am lying in bed trying not to puncture

myself like a tyre, a slow leak. My mother is never driven to

school and once she forgets I exist for hours. I'm a child in a

woman suit. I was thinking of ways to not get crumbs in the

bed. You know I'm talking about suicide, don't you. I am

talking about suicide. It is at the end of the street I

live on. I'm crawling to walk back to the start.

Landslide

I am her reflection; she is my reflection.
I was a tiny girl, held between two fingers.

I rolled out sheet music for automatic pianos,
through the holes pricked grass; through my

fingers the ridges slid. The air pushed me down;
the ground came up; she, she, she, was a whis-

perer. Later, a larger girl, I swallowed the
paper, piece, by body, by piece and she lifted

me with her hands, her rough hands, and she sang
out loud. I realised in this instant that I had al-

ways been here with her. Right from the start
when I popped out of the oven, just like this.

Sigourney Weaver

in your dreams

Sigourney Weaver
and the Dream Father

Last night I was some famous guy's lovechild. There was so much
arguing. I felt like a fountain of eyes and ardour and somehow the
reproduction of Marie Antoinette's estate he had in the backyard
seemed just one farm animal too much. *You* put on the maid outfit
and feed the lambs until dusk; I've got too much thinking to do.

Sigourney Weaver calls me up sometimes to talk. I'm at the bottom
of the earth. Down here knitting by the phone. Her voice likes the
ride and I don't know anyone who knows her from 'up top'. She
likes to talk as if I was the future and she was the past and I give her
mysterious updates on things that are out of her grasp.

Her caboose keeps choo-chooing all through awards ceremonies
where I'm a seat-filler. I know she made that shot from *Alien
Resurrection* where she just tosses the ball over her head. I've seen
her hands. She's seen my pet rabbit. It evens out in the end. We don't
say good night. She just puts the phone away.

The Dream Father wears hats and spurs and sometimes cream silk
stockings tied at his thighs with pale blue ribbons. Breakfast was
a meal seldom worth the effort of dressing. And the pet lambs in
the kitchen went knock-kneed across the floor. His pastoral fantasy
extends to marble countertops and the scent of lanolin.

I whisper to Sigourney Weaver of the Dream Father. Her voice is nutty
with irritation, a hint of cinnamon. She says: '*I'm* the past remember!'
and I hear the handset roll across her countertop and into the sink.
She turns the tap on me in a rush of static and out in the backyard I
hear the Dream Father confessing in a yell: 'It was brioche! Brioche!'

Sigourney Weaver
and I go to bed

Sigourney Weaver flew me some place on what seemed a too small
aeroplane. We didn't talk about her appearance in *Avatar*. The Papyrus
got between us: a font of discontent. She held my hand inside her shirt
and said that she just wanted me to hold her up. I had a potato gun
in my back pocket. She passed the tuber.

After landing we arrived at a white bed. It seemed as tall as she was to
me: a more dumpling-sized human. There were steps around the edges
and the middle was a long marshmallow cloudland in the style of my
home country. I could see her foggy outline reflected in the ceiling.
Her flannelette pyjamas were covered in the faces of dogs.

'This is where we go to bed,' she said. I looked up into her size-nine eyes.
'But, I'm more of a cat person?' This was just like going out with the forty-
two-year-old butch I dated when I was twenty-one. A lot of determined
looks and short phrasing. But she was already up on the mountainy
pillowtop and a long, slender arm loomed at me. The life rope of

a completely different social class. This place was no Dream Father
mansion, but it sure had something going for it. *I was lying in bed with you.*
It was a Thursday. Outside the white noise said it was summer and the cicadas
were okay with that. It had been clear weather for almost ten days. Standing in
the sun a person could be

described as hot. But I'm not allowed to write letters in bed, says Sigourney.
The ink will make a mess of the linen. So I lie there composing in my head.
In bed with Sigourney Weaver. In bed with you. She can palm a
basketball. You're more of a music man than a sports fan. Sigourney
Weaver and I go to bed. All I can think of is you.

Sigourney Weaver
buys property in Aro Valley

Sigourney Weaver started by looking on Trade Me. I'd given her that tip and she tucked it away in her incomprehensible, nesty head. We visit houses together. She always goes and stands staring off into the backyard, if it has one. I try to piece together whether the house will stand up if she buys it. Is there room for her egg chair? Will she fit

through the doorways? Real estate agents are lap dogs in the presence of the great and fearless Sigourney Weaver. She actually takes one onto her knee for a cuddle in a house they show us on the top of Mount Victoria. She pats his little back and he runs off and brings back his phone. Sigourney Weaver isn't into ostentatious

displays of wealth. This house has too much glass. Someone has to clean that you know. He calls and calls and calls until he is standing on his hind legs, his little tail flapping. 'I've found a house in Aro Valley that might be what you're looking for!' Sigourney Weaver asks for the address and leaves him behind. He pants a little with separation

anxiety. I hope the sofa will be safe without us. The sofa hopes it will be safe without us. Sigourney Weaver and I get the bus across town and back up into the Valley. She likes the trolleys, even though we stop twice to let the driver reattach us to the overhead wires. I pay for both of us with my Snapper card and Sigourney Weaver likes to

act as if it wasn't $1.60 and I'm not the small fry. So I also buy us peacherines at the fruiterer. We dribble juice up the street to the address. The house is all veranda and overgrown outside. Even in drought conditions the backyard is a dark, dank tangle. Sigourney Weaver takes out her chequebook and starts writing it down.

Sigourney Weaver
and I rent a movie

Sigourney Weaver doesn't like those chain-store movie rental places.
She likes a stack. She likes photocopied covers and a documentary section
that howls at the moon. She's not wearing a three-wolf sweater; she's just
in the movies so she's in the movies if you know what I mean. Sigourney
Weaver walked down to Aro Video with me.

We passed the thousands of students moving in and out of the street on
the same day. There were dads with trailers or trucks or trucks and trailers
or just dads. Not fathers. And mattresses. We went to the mattresses on
the mattresses. Outside St Vinnie's someone had left a soft toy shaped
like a sheep. Sigourney Weaver rubbed it looking for

lanolin. Through the double doors the staircase creaked in all the usual
places. Rob was on the counter. Sigourney Weaver wasn't in disguise. She
was in fashion, which is the same thing anyway. I always aimlessly browse
the new releases wanting something to walk into my fingers. Or I stare at
the TV section hoping to realise a new state of

being. The transformation of my elastic, floating self's energy into a
television series that will be able to be watched for the first time, repeatedly.
Sigourney Weaver said I should stop self-actualising and start helping.
There's a list. Sigourney Weaver is a woman of complicated desires and
I am here to decipher the omens. As a first

step I read the creases of the backs of her knees. This isn't a day for a
just-missed-the-90s cheerleading comedy. Nor is it the day for charismatic
reimagining of a time when men were stencils and women were baked
in ramekins. Crumbs fall out of her clothing and immediately I know
what to do. 'We'll have *Starship Troopers*, please.'

I take ecstasy with
Sigourney Weaver

A week later and it's mother-daughter moving day. In my living room
Sigourney Weaver and I have taken ecstasy and our necks are sweaty
from the hour-long hug we've been having. I lean to my left and fan the
gap between us. Outside Audi after Audi drops its cargo of high ponytails
and cloud bedding. I was almost run over in the street

buying lemonade by a coterie of matriarchs driving in convoy. All their
coifs stirring absently in the breeze coming through their wide-open
sunroofs. At this point I am the sunroof. Sigourney is the breeze and the
hairdos. We are both connected to our nascent development into the
mothers of second-years, leaving the halls to

find independence in a flat that may have more mould than cooking.
My empty nest shivers with a premonition. I always feel this first in my
thighs. The gravitational thrust of my blood makes them seem pneumatic.
Sigourney Weaver always laughs at me here. She is to laughter what the
Wilhelm scream is to screaming. Once you hear

something enough are you actually hearing the sound or is your muscle
memory remembering you remembering the memory of hearing it for
the first time in 1951? Take that interiority. I've had you pegged since the
moment you threw that two-headed axe. Sigourney Weaver drops my
iPod after switching the music to

'Keep the Streets Empty for Me'. She's trying to make me cry. The screen
is cracked and the lyrics unlock me. I'm the apartment she had in Brooklyn,
it had twelve locks on the door and they had to be opened in sequence.
Sigourney Weaver has nimble fingers and a lock-pick kit in her handbag,
hidden in the lining between two sheets of lead.

Sigourney Weaver
and I come down

Coming down with Sigourney Weaver is a song I sing to myself. It is
much like 'The Girl from Ipanema' which has been relegated to elevator
music though it did win a Grammy. Sigourney Weaver has been nominated
for three Emmys, which are not to be confused with Grammys. Sigourney
Weaver holds a tune like she holds bannisters. In the

middle where Stan Getz is usually playing his wispy sax, Sigourney Weaver
and I are lying on her veranda watching the light on the sharp contours of
the roof. 'Baaah baba baaah baaah bababa baaah.' At this stage I'm always a
non-Newtonian fluid. Sigourney Weaver taps my shoulder and I'm a person.
Once she stops touching me I subside into

the custard you recognise. A companionable spooning situation forms
organically. I have to be the little spoon simply because my dimensions
are more pedestrian. More person than custard, I care not for individual
minutes. If you imagine time, you don't just imagine the queue at the
supermarket. Sigourney Weaver imagining time spreads

her hands above her head and lets the tree canopy show between her
fingers. It is leaves and ferns with borders made of the difference between
now and the sky. Sigourney Weaver rolls me into the crook of her arm and
we look at her cuticles and the evidence of the Milky Way starting to appear
as bright spots in the backs of our eyes.

As custard, Sigourney Weaver leans across me, and places her mouth in
the same space my mouth occupies. As a person I know this is a kiss.
The romantic dyad claims a lot of territory for itself, selfishly. We know
as a platonic dyad this kissing is kissing itself. Sigourney Weaver is the soft
inside of a bread roll, split apart with your fingers.

Sigourney Weaver and I go through Suicide Tuesday together

Sigourney Weaver and I held hands a lot on the day that was Suicide Tuesday but actually was just a Wednesday. We were depleted and easily overheated while the lakes of serotonin in our brains slowly refilled. Sigourney Weaver was a first-time MDMA user and seemed to find comfort in knowing this couldn't last forever. She asked me to

repeat the story of my friend who went to the doctor after his first time because he'd never felt so depressed in his life and worried for his mental health. At least she wasn't having that conversation, she said. Sigourney Weaver didn't much like doctors. And doctors don't always like actors. And I only act like I like doctors so that they don't

immediately pick me as the hostile, disruptive type 'cause you can't give them any excuse to give you bad care. They will certainly take it. Sigourney Weaver said she couldn't believe no one told my friend this would happen to him. I said no one could believe he didn't know. Wasn't being alive in the 90s enough? I hoped being alive in the 90s

was enough. Thank various deities I was no longer a teenager. Being a teenager was being trapped in a panic room you didn't know how to operate except it was your brain and it was impossible to tell where you were at any one time. There was no Google Maps with GPS that could find you as long as you had reception, when I was fifteen.

There's never been an instruction manual. I'm sure all the doctors you know are good people. I just can't quite get over how they never seem to respect my opinion. Sigourney Weaver says she would like to be acknowledged as the subject matter expert for her body due to her overwhelming experience and qualifications.

Sigourney Weaver helps me
out of some feelings (not pants)

Sometimes when I consider the inside of my brain it seems like it must
be honeycomb not flesh. Or the symmetrical petals of a complex flower.
Sigourney Weaver always looks like she wants to tell me to go run around
outside. Or read a book. Stop trying to make noodles in your skull. Ramen
was never meant for this. Sigourney

Weaver knows I have a therapist but likes to add corn and butter to the
broth anyway. It's always Hokkaidō styles around here. Ezo or Yezo or
Yeso, or Yesso. You can take the miso out of the ramen but you can't take
the ramen out of the miso without putting it in your mouth. These feelings
are ancient and naked mole rats

conditioned to darkness and not feeling pain. You can try to stop them
but they keep on digging with their teeth for the tubers to feed their
queen. Sigourney Weaver is my queen in the eusocial utopia of my dreams.
It is a pity I'm the only worker trying to make this happen. That includes
Sigourney Weaver. She's not keen to give birth

to litters. But Sigourney Weaver knows how to undress my feelings as if
they were a small child. Always that tug to get the neck-hole over the slightly
too-large head. She folds the arm expertly across the front of the body to
release the limb from its sleeve. She is unafraid of their tiny, soft bodies.
The feelings, they are naked after she

touches them. And once they're naked it is easier to sweep them into the
current of a fast-flowing river. Feet first little feelings, feet first. Sigourney
Weaver blows air out of her mouth in what may be a horsey manner but I
don't interrupt her to say that. She's dangling the last troublesome jerk-
feeling by her fingers over the gap. And splash.

Sigourney Weaver and I renegotiate our boundaries

Sigourney Weaver comes to my house today, dressed as a mime. She's all curls and black suspenders, which she snaps and snaps and snaps. I have so many feelings, Sigourney Weaver, they can't even fit all inside my body and they are pushing their little hands through my thin, tin skin. They stretch for the outside. I am no Rin Tin Tin!

I wasn't rescued and then put to work. You're the perform-mancer here Sigourney Weaver, you divine my substance through your art. Sigourney Weaver just looks at me as she rides a mimed bike whilst remaining in the same physical space. She does a jaunty elbow flick and winks. We have to talk, Sigourney Weaver. I'm a mentally ill,

married, chronically ill, queer woman with two feet underground and you're dressed as a mime and not speaking on the day I broke the candle we carved together in my image. Sigourney Weaver mimes the outline of a box and rattles what must be a set of window bars. She's making a joke about a ball and chain because I'm queer in the

marriage too. This is no time for jokes, Sigourney Weaver. We're discussing the liminal interaction of our fleshy meat sacks with our emotional cores. I'm not a boxed companion that you add water and 90s movies to any time you need a little extra amity from someone who doesn't work you too hard. Sigourney Weaver pratfalls down the

steps into the lounge, where she can barely stretch her form out in a straight line because of all the angles and furniture. So she curls into a little mime ball, in a little mime boat in the middle of a treacherous mime ocean. Sigourney Weaver extends her arm to me, a plea. From three steps above I throw a mint-flavoured Life Saver into her mouth.

Sigourney Weaver and I play
video games at Wizards

Sigourney Weaver from 1979 and me from 2003 go to play video games
at Wizards in the mid-1980s. We take a bag of old-style twenty-cent pieces
to weigh us down, even though we will have to turn them into tokens.
The difficulty of time travel is continuity. This Sigourney Weaver isn't
even really *the* Sigourney Weaver yet. She's barely even

Ripley. At this point I was wearing dresses and pigtails and crushing on
Ms. Thompson. And then in 2003 I was like a burst fruit. I remember
peeking inside Wizards on the caterpillar walk to the library, a sweaty
little hand in my little hand. The inside of the arcade looked like velvet
darkness. Go roll around in there with a handful of

money and the sound of Pac-Man and his endless hunger. I can't remember
anything about Wizards except for the sign now. And of course what video
game machines from the 80s looked like. I'm making this up with
Sigourney Weaver although if we're time travelling I guess this is the reality.
Or this is all happening at once

like a collapsing universe and it doesn't matter what it looks like because
it never looked like anything anyway because it was gone before it was here.
Like Caffiends, which exists in me only through stories of older goths but
is just at the corner of the block if we care to take a walk. I would have hung
out there had I figured out I was a

person in time to actually do something as a teenager other than listen
to Tori Amos and live under hair. Don't forget about The Coachman. It's on
the same street and my family ate steak there in good times. Gloucester
Street. With the library it had pretty much everything. Sigourney Weaver
loses another life, another token.

Sigourney Weaver seduces
me with the purchase of a van

Sigourney Weaver knows how I feel about practicality. Flat shoes. Fold-out couches. Capacious handbags. Washable knit fabric. She taps into the sap of my phloem and detects the nutritious material there with her rostrum. Just say a few words in a row. Fold-down seats. Carpet-lined interior. USB-capable stereo. Double drink-holder.

Sigourney Weaver sits outside my house in her new van, revving the engine and opening and closing all the doors. She's performing the love song of the van devotee. She takes the couch from my lounge and puts it in the van. Then she takes the couch out and puts it back in my lounge. I think this is a metaphor, Sigourney Weaver.

Later she comes back with the van full of boxes. She unloads them in the street, climbs onto the roof of the van and theatrically falls into the boxes I hadn't known were empty until the weight of her bones and blood compacted the cardboard. Sigourney Weaver is holding up traffic but with a shake of her curled kinda-mullet and the extension

of her limbs to walking she's signing autographs and convincing courier drivers and the guy who always drives too fast down our street that this is something worth their time. I stand by our letterbox watching her with the van at her feet like a faithful steed. This would be a Western and I would be the corseted sex-worker-teacher-wife

if only we had time. She's the straight shooter with the crooked grin wearing leather pants and a linen shirt. Her spurs are heart-shaped and the lanyard around her neck has some of my hair plaited, under glass. Sigourney Weaver pulls the brim of her hat low, bending at the waist, the courier driver forgotten. 'Afternoon, ma'am,' she says.

Sigourney Weaver gets citizenship and goes to a ceremony

You're encouraged to wear formal clothing from your culture for the citizenship ceremony. Sigourney Weaver says she can probably get that yellow mech-suit if she tries. I'm not sure that's what they mean, Sigourney Weaver. But the other choice is that fucking awful 70s/80s-style bikini underwear you were always wearing to at once titillate and

confirm the delicate vulnerability of your meat sack. Your thighs and shoulders aside, they made you all nipples and a suggestion of labial folds. And if I know anything, Sigourney Weaver, it's that underwear is not appropriate formal wear, no matter what the director says. 'I'll just wear a suit. I'll just wear a suit.' I know Sigourney Weaver has to

swear allegiance to the queen. I am not sure Sigourney Weaver has yet figured out she has to swear allegiance to the queen. Born here, it's just assumed I'm okay with that old bird who looks a lot like Lucian Freud in the painting he did of her. Part self-portrait, part true record of a wrinkly monarch. Here then gone. Sigourney Weaver can't

be a citizen in two places even though she's a citizen in two places. She came here on a boat but no one gets out slurs to talk about her in the newspaper. The colour of her money is whatever colour the government made it and everyone likes it that way. Just like the way the queen is the richest welfare recipient I know of. No one tells her

off for stabling the corgis or getting a new dress every time she has to leave the house to break a bottle of wine. Not to mention if she spends all her cash on sherry and speed, the crowd goes silent. Sigourney Weaver waits for my steam to run out. 'Shame I have to swear allegiance to the queen instead of swearing it to you.'

Sigourney Weaver
and the impregnation

Sigourney Weaver has an adult child. She's past the crying and the feeding and the night walking and has moved on to interviewing boyfriends and discussing career trajectories. But for some reason she has a tab in her browser devoted to cotton onesies and has been asking about locally made wooden toys. Sigourney Weaver is

considering an impregnation. My womb has been implanted with the idea of never being implanted with anything. This has been the most effective implantation of its life. My womb and I carry on daily together with this understanding. It treats me with respect if I respect its wishes. I respect its wishes. Sigourney Weaver starts to look at me

as if she may not be going to respect my wishes for very much longer. Sigourney Weaver, the face hugger. We've gone full circle now. I lie awake in bed awaiting her inevitable offer to turkey baste my insides with acceptable sperm. My fears turn out to be unfounded. The next day I discover Sigourney Weaver in a shed with wires and a

row of tiny rubber faces. She's the metal mother dreaming her android baby to sleep. As she fiddles with wires and artificial skin she coos and croons. 'Sigourney Weaver,' I say, 'Don't you have a complex relationship with androids?' 'I see where you're coming from. I hear what you're saying. But I quite liked that last one. She made choices I

approved of. Plus she had that jack in her arm disguised as a freckle. I really appreciated the detail and the utility.' There is a pregnant pause. 'Plus, I know you aren't getting knocked up for anyone. Not even me.' Ah, Sigourney Weaver. Knower of hearts and minds. My womb is a derelict house and you want to spray-paint your name on it.

Sigourney Weaver
in the womb

This is the point where I tell you that Sigourney Weaver is one year, eleven months and three days younger than my mother. When Sigourney Weaver was incubating in a womb of her own, my mother was learning to walk and talk just like her composition doll. In the womb Sigourney Weaver was destined to be a Susan. My mother's

composition doll, also called Susan, cries if you tip her up at the right angle. In the womb Sigourney Weaver started the cycle of everything. She wrote a list of tasks on a small sheet of paper ripped from one of those little notebooks you get when you start school and used the pencils they gave out at Pizza Hut in the 80s. If you were lucky it

came with a pencil sharpener too. Sigourney Weaver does without but is careful of the lead. I'm not sharing the list with you because it's not mine to share. But suffice to say there were some things on there that would be of interest to you if I were to share it. Sigourney Weaver lights a cigarette and sucks on it thoughtfully as the list and pencil

float around in the amniotic fluid. At this point I'm not even close to existence. But here I am, watching. It's just a spaceman cigarette so you can relax. No mothers were harmed in the making of this, except perhaps my own. You mother your own mother and she mothers you. And in that mothering you're mothering yourself the way you wanted

to be mothered. My mother always had food on the table and made clothes for all the bodies in the house including my dolls. My mother wasn't prepared for me. I was an unfolding box of tricks that just never ended. I was a boy in a girl suit and a depressed hat in a rain storm. Sigourney Weaver, she started out small and got bigger.

I birth Sigourney Weaver's android baby

When the time comes to turn the baby on, Sigourney Weaver asks
me to birth it. 'I want it to come into the world the usual way.' I nod
and suggest a slightly less literal solution. We spend the rest of the
afternoon creating a blanket fort in the living room with a vaginal
canal leading out into the rest of the house. I'm not sure how far I can

get into this. But I find myself downloading a track of someone's
heartbeat off the internet to play on the stereo. Sigourney Weaver wants
me to mix it into a recording of the sea for, you know, the realism.
Somehow I feel like this whole exercise is leading to me actually giving
birth in approximately nine months. Finally I could rest

my hands on my stomach and if someone asked me when I was due
I could tell them rather than alienating them by admitting to fatness
instead of fecundity. Sigourney Weaver tugs the red woollen blanket we
have repurposed into the birth canal into place and stares at me letting
me know I'm not pulling my weight. Because this is a ritual I

light candles. In the wobbling light, Sigourney Weaver and I take the
android baby into the fort and lie there together as three pieces.
Sigourney Weaver tucks some hair behind my ear and lifts my head
to rest it on her arm. The android baby is between us in a red and white
striped onesie. I suspect the name of the child will eventually be

revealed as Toby. I would prefer a fruit name. Or something even
weirder than that. Perhaps we could call the baby an anagram of all the
letters of our combined names. Or perhaps I will finally get to name
someone Wolfgang. Wolfy in the diminutive. Wolfgang Weaver because
everyone knows alliterative names are basically better.

Sigourney Weaver confronts
the limits of desire

Sigourney Weaver tells me that desire has a hard edge. The end. The limit it enforces by virtue of its own inevitability. She's been reading the internet again. Sigourney Weaver says that our bodies are wishes made from DNA and that time and time again we defeat ourselves with our limited thinking. Always imagining edges. The edge of desire

is only there because we put it there. And we put it there because we can't make sense of a world where we could desire and act in equal measure. Trust Sigourney Weaver to get me tied up in knots without any rope. Not even the tiniest string around my finger. I like a boundary, Sigourney Weaver. I like clear statements and small words. I

like knowing if my heart is going to make it another round before it has to tap out or someone rings a bell. I'll spit all that blood and saliva into a bucket before I get back up off this chair and then we can go another round. This time we're discussing kissing. Forgive me, Sigourney Weaver, for I have kissed. It has been twelve hours since I last

kissed someone and a week since I last kissed two someones you didn't know. Sigourney Weaver tells me she's not angry, she's just disappointed. I tell her that I will kiss whomever I want to kiss, at the time and location of my choosing. This is the original argument. We pretend to hold hands. Our pretend hand-holding creates pretend

hand-sweat. Here's an edge of desire, Sigourney Weaver, that you have placed inside my body though it is actually inside your own. There are edges we can sneak through and edges we can rub away and edges, like hedges that trap us in thorns and leaves and mazes made out of corn. We are all just one body. We are all pretending to hold hands.

Sigourney Weaver
and I break up

Sigourney Weaver and I sit in the living room. She folds her hands
on her knees demurely, holding herself like a package of teeth. We are
breaking up like an ice shelf in spring. There are loud cracks as the
ice shelf calves and the majority of the berg sinks below the surface to
be heralded by its small, white peak. Sigourney Weaver and I attempt

the phrases of romantic disentanglement. 'It's not you, it's me.' 'We've
grown apart.' 'It's not me, it's you.' 'I can't do this any longer.' 'You left
the cap off the toothpaste.' 'I've met someone else.' 'I feel like we should
see other people.' 'The romance has left the building.' 'We're better
friends than lovers.' 'You love your hair more than me.'

Sigourney Weaver cocks an eyebrow at me and divides us up into a
room of items arranged by colour in the style of Das Werkbundarchiv
– Museum der Dinge in Berlin. I am all the yellow things because of
the colour of my home. Sigourney Weaver is all the red things because
of the colour of her embarrassed blush. She has unlocked

the cabinet of soap. She has picked the soap up in her hands. She has
melted them into a heart shape destroying their singularity. She then
snaps the heart in two and passes me one of the halvings. 'We can't
break up, love bug. There is no way to divide our souls in two like soap.
I'm not snapping you out of it. You're not leaving me here.'

How Sigourney Weaver of Sigourney Weaver to just end a conversation
with an imperative. 'This is a fake-up.' 'Were we even trying?' 'I've
remade the world from scratch.' Sigourney Weaver stands me up like
a bowling pin and wraps her arms around me. 'This is the best break-
up I've ever had,' she says over the top of my head of air. 'The best.'

Sigourney Weaver
brushes my hair

Sigourney Weaver has found the me with hip-length hair. She has
reduced her into a relaxed pulp and is brushing her hair. Sigourney
Weaver rests the hair across her hand and brushes down and through
it from scalp to end. Long, slow repeated strokes. It's like she's racking
up points that I remember here in the future as it puts a kink

in time. The rule is we don't talk about time travel. The rule is that
I'm me wherever I'm me. If Sigourney Weaver's not with me am I with
Sigourney Weaver? If I'm with you this time, will she notice? This
hair existed in 2005, 2006 and briefly in 2007. This hair has known
me and you and her and Sigourney Weaver brushes the strands as if

they represent time itself. This is a slow dance when we were both
sixteen at a ball neither of us went to but somewhere we're in ball
dresses letting our stomachs touch and our arms loop around each
other like the empty space in a doughnut. You go through time as a
progression until it's not a progression and you are hurtling through

it like a hunger. I have never tasted time as good as this time. It is
better than cheeseburgers or matcha frappés or the entire twelve-
course vegetarian Korean meal Soon cooked for me once. The jelly was
made from agar and elderflower soda and in my mouth it was a slow
deterioration of bubbles. This time is better than a slow deterioration

of bubbles. I always go to love when surprised. Here I am descending
a tower of stone steps, my head floating through the classical
movements of love. Allegro to adagio to scherzo and a return to allegro
where my heart rate is at slight elevation because you've kissed me,
Sigourney Weaver, as a tower of wood, silk and stone.

Sigourney Weaver and I correspond only via email

Sigourney Weaver only writes to me from gotlegs1997@hotmail.com, her very own little anachronism. She never quite got into AOL.com or having her own domain, though of course she has her own domain. She comes to email like a villain. It's not quite a letter; it's not quite a poem. It's a set of signs and a wild signature. We write to

each other like the recently bereaved. We don't talk about the not talking about but the not talking about is all we want to talk about. There's a shape in the living room like a beast of burden under cover and there's a little song playing outside that makes the ache of a childhood never quite held onto. Sigourney Weaver is in Rome and

then she's in Synecdoche, New York and then she's in her home in Aro Valley, tapping at a keyboard and mouse, clicking send. Her mouth clicks and bends. Her mother and my mother sit down at a table and drink tea. Sigourney Weaver, this isn't a patch on the times we were together but I'll take it. I am the regurgitation of my days and the

thoughts I have while walking. Sigourney Weaver takes the rubbish out and brings it back in again and then writes me a shopping list and ends it in a rush. We are all the harakeke clicking in the wind. I am refreshing my inbox and refreshing my inbox then turning all my notifications off. I lie on a single bed and stare up into the sun and

Simon buries a dead kāruhiruhi that just seemed to fall out of the sky. When I fell out of the sky my neck was not cradled by strands of wild grass my body held in blackberry vines. My feet did not fold up like leather purses and water did not bead on my chest. I landed with a printed email clutched in my hand, no heed for warnings.

Sigourney Weaver becomes
the witch of the block

Aro Valley is a collection of glass tubes and tumble-down old shacks,
the past and the future coming together in a shambles. Children
squabble on what we wish were hoverboards but are still just
skateboards. Sigourney Weaver has transformed into a hedge witch.
Her house, so charmingly overgrown when I was half the age I am

now, is one rotund hedge with a chimney. Sigourney Weaver herself
is a reclusive spiral perm with a set of shoulders hung beneath it.
On Tuesdays I take the almost centenarian a little lemon cake in a
little cardboard box and bag of groceries leaning heavily towards facon,
bread and milk. I crawl through the hedge and look out over the

street from the side where the children's projectiles land and the
beer bottles collect. I never saw this side of my own hedge-witch house
on Lichfield Street in 1980s Christchurch. Between a car yard and
a bearing shop, a two-second walk from the vehicle-testing station,
over the back of the small local rag. I would shut my eyes and ride

my bike as fast as I could past it. Or maybe I would look only at the
rusted roof of the curved veranda. The creeper would brush its fingers
against me if at all possible. Sigourney Weaver says thank you each
time by calling me by my full name and telling me that I'm more
trouble than I'm worth. This is classic hedge-witch fare. It's like a

menu where you'd choose the same dish every time. 'Old woman,'
I say. 'Old woman, I know that little lemon cake is the light of your life.'
She twists her head and a wry shape comes to her lips. I clean her
kitchen and trim her toenails and take out last week's trash. Sigourney
Weaver shuts her eyes for just a minute on the couch.

The Run-Around

And many-gendered mothers of the heart say: *Just because you have enemies does not mean you have to be paranoid.* They insist, no matter the evidence marshaled against their insistence: *There is nothing you can throw at me that I cannot metabolize, no thing impervious to my alchemy.*

—Maggie Nelson, *The Argonauts*

Give up

There's a direct line to the beginning of a god when I give up against you. A small spark in the universe made of proton gradients and the fine mist of your breath condensing against me. The beam of our gaze holds firm under my toes. You've set me five flick-flacks and a back handspring back-tuck to which the beam responds with gentle flexing. It turns out my weight is more or less inconsequential to the fingers of your right hand. And your left hand holds me flat by the belly, a pin. The phasing we are together is a waveform where I am the peak and you are the valley. We are edge to edge like all good risks and measures. We are shearing off into cracking and shaking, the sweat of time and thighs. We raise our eyes skyward. Or we raise our eyes to the roof. Or we raise our eyes into each other. The beam is white with chalk. Its ten centimetres seem like a gift when you stand on it to do a back walkover. It narrows when you're in the air, your legs tucked to untuck later into the firm base of your body. You tell me I will vaporise when your hands are on me and your face connects with mine. I believe you because you are drawing me into shapes and those shapes are windows and those windows open into fields of summer grass that are mid-thigh when I walk out into the hot air. Your weight on top of me crushes flowers beneath us.

The heel of your palm

The eyes in your face reach out of you across the room to me. The rows your
fingers make through each other press back, hard into me. The heel of your
palm pushing against the breastbone of my imagination. I am the glare of
the sun too closely looked at. You stand beside me and enjoy the experience.
You can see inside my body from that point of view but never look. I under-
stand what people mean when they say they can't find me. It's such a calm
feeling your eyes on my face to lips to eyes only. You find a different me
in a completely different location and tell no one about it. What is it to be
respected so completely it feels like disappearing. My arms are rubbed out
by a comically large eraser then it moves down my body to my chest and half
my torso disappears. As this scene plays out your hand cradles my occipital
bone and you fold in half to take your lips to mine. It is the lightest touch
that's possible to still feel. I accidentally fantasise about your fingers inside
me. The heel of your palm against the pubic bone of my imagination. I've never
thought this about anyone else. Your hands wrapped around mine to slow my
conversational momentum and I am stuck on it. Slowed permanently by the
shape of your nail beds and what it is like to be wrapped up in another body
leading you out of yourself and back to yourself. The outside can't find me.
I can't find me, here.

The cap of my shoulder

In the dream you are rolled up against me. Your face pressed deeply into the cap of my shoulder. Your arm across my ribcage falls through my bodies as they are layered against one another. It is a substantial escalation in intimacy. We are naked in a dream bed. The sheets trap us. You did once lift me to my toes, into a hug and pressed your mouth to my ear to tell me you loved me. It was 3 a.m., an acceptable confession. And you've looked at me with your eyes before. But I wake up with guilt after this dream of us. It takes me all day to wiggle out of the nest, the maze, the rumpled bed sheets and even then I will have to look you in the eye soon and not remember the nature of skin against skin. You're leaving. This time it's just wine and perhaps a touch of adrenaline. But your arms take me in again and you say those words. To make a spell stronger you repeat it. In the dream your body was a weight that was like a thunder coat. The soft tautness of safety. The encouraging weight of love.

Hot spit

My mouth fills with hot spit. A man's face containing intention. A cartoon eye suspended in a field of white. My mouth fills with hot spit. You are hot and even against me and I can see all your flat planes. You're a series of notes separated by gulps of heat or my hand grabbed out of air. Or my name. And I am a tide. Or I am a metronome on largo. You'll wait for a click in a captured eternity. Then we will be liquid over a flame. Or we're coming back together in time. Repeat the catchphrase. Tap out the password onto the tabletop like you made it your piano. My mouth sinks. The room spins on an axis. I have taken enough stimulants that I'm just all and only feeling. The outside is quiet. And I'm all feeling. All nothing. All knowing. A pyramid on a pyramid on the muscled backs of champion cheerleaders. The run of muscle against their spines. The gentle head-flick of joy. You come together into what is really just a chain of vibration. Let me send up a tray to heaven. I will roll you in my mouth. I'll roll you against my breast. I'll roll you with the dark ring around my iris. Let me roll you, this once. But just when the sun rises I'll split you apart, into pieces, and leave you inside the circle, alone with your thoughts.

The vermilion line

You ride along my body in a single curl to rest your mouth on my neck to drive it to the base of my skull behind my ear. You whisper sound into me like I'm a cup. You ask questions that seek no reply. It's in control. It's out of control. It's my word against yours. It's the cycle of pleading that rolls from your big eyes down through your deltoids to your fingertips. This communication feels silent. Two tides running through each other. Two moons. Two moans. You hang off me with your teeth gripping my bottom lip. You slide your hands inside my chest and leave them there wrapped in ribs, wrapped in something only you can feel. The small life of loneliness unfolds within you as I stand in front of you. But you shift against me like I am seeing you from another angle. Like you've rotated around the sun enough times you've worn away the edges. I will not draw the attention. I will not pull the focus. I will not sink the ship. It's my will and your will and our will and a slow tension we feel as a negotiation that happens with only our mouths. That first time we're one body is the best moment of all moments. But we're two bodies. I'm five bodies. The air makes six. All the numbers lie down beside me and shake themselves to sleep. The nip you took to my neck stings. I'm a full body graze just thinking about the shapes of you.

I invite myself inside

You have not kissed me. I have not been kissed. The night approaches with the sound of starlings finding roost. And you have still not kissed me. I kissed myself in the mirror of myself to find the thread that connected me to the place where I knew what it meant to be someone after their own heart. Or hearts in the same shape. The shape of a heart is the fist. Gender is a cloud where no one exists as a real thing. We are all just the skin that covers our bodies underneath the clothes that cover us up. I've told you since I was eighteen that I'm not the same person I looked like I would be when my clothes aren't there. I've told you that the outside and the inside are not the same place even in a human body. You don't have to say my name. I don't have to know anything about you. Just say some of those words out loud and out loud and out loud. The horizon pretends to be flat because we can't believe the shape. My shape shifts as it is perceived. I'm perceived through several different moments in time at the same time. You know how to freeze-frame, I know how to say abracadabra forwards and backwards and into the space above your head. Your head above me is hard to look at. Like everything that I've ever looked at I forget it only to remember it later. In the secret mythology of a self I write down everything. It rolls through me like the barrel of a zoetrope spinning and spinning and the horse moves inside me. And I am the horse. And the horse rolls its eyes right out of its head. I have kissed you but I don't remember. I have kissed you and I remember each dizzying moment. I have not kissed you and looking at your mouth in the dim light of dusk is invitation enough. I invite myself inside.

Low boughs

I am made of metal and light and the sun knows it is me looking backwards over its shoulder you know I just want to be loved in the way that this feeling pours from me out into the daylight my body isn't made of bones and flesh it's made of pressure and stones and the dripping of caves and windows you forget the power of drawing things to you in the speeding up of time different things come now but when it was you oh I loved you but now instead I try to love smaller things like the bees and borage on the stairs and the kingfisher on the powerlines and the young woman who smiled at me on the bus but small things are everywhere and just once I'd like to smooth the air between us again but you leave all oxygen in the past and refuse everything about me and I am refused often enough this only feels like the sliding scale of the natural order of things living and dying and being reborn as something else again and again until your biggest atom is now the smallest atom at the end of the universe and it starts again how strange to have given yourself up for yourself and to find yourself as rested as a small god worshipped between breaths not to say you're a small god but the lines on our faces share something of a similarity like our bodies were meant to be together for five minutes only lips locked hands against chests then we parted like curtains in the morning to let the light in so that we can harvest the fruit bringing the boughs low to the earth I have bent at the knees to reach for the ground only to find that when I stand I'm alone again just like before.

The butter knife

In the reverse ordering of memory I always see me in the light that I've been seen in before. The darkening of middle age where we come to invisibility and mistrust of the prior senses of youth. No one really knows anything but especially when you're young. As a slightly less young person the inevitable disappearing act my face and body performs is still something strange and seeming unexplained. Or a surprise. Money jingles through the entire world and we get shaken through selves that represent the size of our pockets. I grew up very small. The sound and the sound and the sound of the rivers of money echoed through other cities and other worlds and other people. I am the butter knife of this. Such a flat and useless blade until you slide it against the right fat. That things and people end seems impossible given their continuance. How will this minute ever pass. How will you be gone from my life one way or another. We are all ways and ways and always. The exhausting desires inside me reach out and forwards through the spaces between us as over time my breasts soften and disappear. No one told me about all of these things. There's so much I was never told. It is exhausting having to figure it all out for yourself. As I get stronger new muscles appear in me that have appeared and receded before. Strength is a continual practice. It is anything. The daily repetitions and lapses of selves coming and going. I am wild in all the wrong places. And you tell me the names of people I will never know, like facts. I do not pay attention to them. Retention is not my place. I am a thing instead that never forgets a face. A trap. A misery. A spell against invisibility that instead makes me invisible. You make your own choices and they are so small and simple in the moments you make them that they seem so unable to cause damage, so unable to leave you later alone, leave you later less than you were before. Unfortunately, nothing ever grinds to a halt. It just always keeps moving. There is no single truth I can tell you. We end up like this, apart and afar.

To be known

The desire to be known and to be loved anew for old things for the same stories for the brief possibility of transformation. It is an ache that pages through Tinder on the off-chance of seeing something deeper than an Olympic diving pool. Something better than the blurry face of a man unable to see himself as an object. I age and I age and I age and I sit beside someone almost ten years my senior and his skin is so smooth his face held so blank, bar the slight secret smile he sends in my direction when I manage to say something that pulls him out of himself and into the bright downlight of the table. I know him like a small secret. We are a small secret never born. The small tingling barriers of relationships rattle over my skin. Have you made bread and felt the dough become correct. Have you felt the way twenty years can feel like a blink. How does skin work. Will the oxygen that's degrading me now later keep me alive. Why do guitars with the right pedal sound like the way my heart hurt when I was twenty and so lonely I didn't even know how to be friends with myself. In the dark of a bar the dark of the bar feels like life being given to you anew. I said so many things to people I loved in the dark, in this dark. The safety of darkness. Of being unseen and unknown then the blinding rightness of being seen and known. I wouldn't say understood. To understand is to answer the phone and I almost never do that on the first go. Call again.

Completely dry riverbed

In the desert the sand is red and soft and takes the skin off your feet. You open up your bed like a sandwich, crawl under the lettuce and lie near a fire that burns down into the sand. The sky above is blank with stars. You wake into it as waves and run your fingers through them but sleep claws you back until you come up again thinking of dingoes drinking out of cups of water beside heads. That was a story that happened to a head near yours now when it wasn't near your head but still asleep in a swag. The dingoes always want something. That night it was water. Sometimes they take each of your belongings to a safe radius to examine only to be disappointed with every sock and every shoe. A ring around a camp of all your lost belongings, thirty feet out. In the dry riverbed the dogs chase after everything with a keen sense of righteousness anticipating perhaps Terry, a dingo that fell in love with a dog. But who knows the minds of dogs let alone dingoes. And love cannot be explained in any case.

Begin again

Of course I still love you. It's like this. You tell the sea and the sea tells me and then you're all over and under and above the world looking down into a set of eyes with dilated pupils. Time can't reduce that into sand. It's not water. It's not wave and wearing and rocks. But then if we're real this was never the problem. We're not real. We're all just made up on the day, nothing done ahead of time. My mise en place is always done once everything is wound up and done. We'll put it in its place. You put me in my place with a name that's dead. I let the sides of the world collapse around me. A friend in Portugal puts a piece of bread on the ground and I do too. In this moment the world is a sandwich of our own making and we're the quietest collaborators. Let me look at us. Let me look. We'll wave goodbye to each other with our bodies and I'll be a river of waterfalls on my face. I'll be a river of waterfalls over the shape we make together, which is the first shape we made together. All beginnings are endings. I'm holding your hand even when we're not together. This beginning is our very first ending.

Cut

The boat in the middle of the ocean looks up to the full moon. The light and the darkness blend into each other in the shape of a pyramid. It is a brief period of emptiness as the camera shows the waves near me as a blur and the ones further away as a more regular texture. I am both existence and nothing like everything in the world. I ejected half of my life as a magnetic tape, my jaw cracked wide to release it. Here I stand half empty of myself. Half full of myself. I will feed myself into an algorithm and create new selves from the sorting. On the boat deck it's so cold I sneeze myself anew.

I have to dig the splinters out by hand from my hand. I use a safety pin to pop them up out of the skin and then I tweeze the slivers of wood out into the open. I do this four times from the edge of my palm. I gripped a wooden basket and they entered me. I gripped the basket because there was nothing else to do that day but burrow into my own self and the basket followed suit. I am the truth of the matter. The single, solitary voice. I am the frequency of the A above middle C. No one in this room knows I'm the tone to calibrate to. But I just say the same words at 440 Hz. The repeated tone carries true.

The burrow is lined with fur. I am the rabbit plucking my own chest to shelter the smaller selves I've created. I set them free here. When they are loose they are me, but free. Me but much smaller. Me but completely without sight for now. The outside is terrifying to us collectively. We're an organism of many selves, many cells. Living in a body like I am I'm reminded repeatedly of my lack of sovereignty over myself. You're a rabbit. So small, vulnerable to fright, to harm. When his hand grasps my body around my lithe middle I only escape due to luck. I return home to eat my selves to save me from all this.

In the process of ageing I'm $(39 \div 7 = 5.57)$ new heads and $(39 \div 7 = 5.57)$ new handles. I'm still the same axe. I'm still capable of cutting wood in two, into four. I don't know if my handle is smooth. I don't know if it leaves splinters in the palms of those who wield it. I only know the smooth pull of gravity. The logs all cry out at 440 Hz. The bell of my heart rings in sympathy but still, I cut the wood. When the smaller selves are eaten I still need to clear-fell the forests they hid in. The wolves, the monsters, the men hide in the woods too. If I was a match I could burn it apart. But I'm an axe, I cut.

Down

I have finally taken it down. I have put it in a hole in the ground with a wood trap lid. I tap three times on the top and walk away clean. I later shower rhythmically, breathing out my pace. As I stand dripping on the ground, dripping on wood, my body changes shape. It's like watching you perform for me. But this time what you're performing is the recreation of my self without the things I locked in the ground. I can't tell you what I put in there. It is not a complete body of work. I can't say it out loud. My fingers take on a new shape. I lose the weight of my stomach and it comes back to gentleness. My thighs pare back to heavy muscle. My palms are no longer square and the lines separate out into a head and heart. When it is done no one will know it is me. No one could pick me by scar or by face. I pick myself like fresh flowers. Snipping my stems diagonally I lie down between sheets made out of the things I used to think. I am heavy now as a canvas blanket held in your arms, draped down your body. I lie diagonally across your heart against the warm weight of us. I'll cut myself up for the air. Paper pieces. Confetti. A single word. Together in the middle of the night our bodies move closer, sighing.

You are a horrible goose

In the common land inside the city running through this place I think of streamers catching the wind as I find myself holding onto something that doesn't exist any longer. In service there is no longer safety only the quiet of something very wrong. I thought it was love like I think so many things are love and it is only now I know that love is a conversation and I have just been talking to myself alone in an empty room. A pattern repeated with smaller and smaller variations until the spiralling bone at its centre is revealed. When it is ended for you the time seems longer, shorter, wasted, better, inevitable. The deep emptiness of being let down by your own self in your own time. I sleep through layers of consciousness dreaming into past selves and past lives and the certainty of nothing and no one. We end each day face up to the sky and it does nothing for us until we are prepared to become the horrible goose in our own lives. I will be the most joyous goose of my own heart and hound many of you in the village. Put the rake in the lake. Honk your heart out. Unfettered by who I was before. Set free by stealing your bell for myself.

Before you arrive

You are here before you arrive. The feeling of you in the spaces before you're in the spaces. There's a part of you wandering. Don't make it seem like anything could happen. I avoid looking at you. There are entire songs that are call and response. Entire choirs. I call instinctively and you respond quietly, with complete plausible deniability. Or do you call and I respond. Is it both. Is it nothing. The currents of human interaction are wild and wide and we're both trying not to make eye contact. I turn into a completely different thing when under the grasp of sexual tension. I have been a dead thing, a bug, a husk, dust for months upon months. I want honesty but speaking openly tethers us to the ground. All I want is to pull up the tent pegs and let the fly loose. I want to see the sky from its own perspective. That's what a kiss can feel like. Or the touch of a hand where it wasn't before. A static charge will crack between us. No one says a word, least of all me. No one will say a word. The bright orange fly from the tent of my heart flaps like a dying seabird.

There is no good ending

It starts here. You were born today. And later you died. And even later we were still here. The endless running tides and the wind that shakes the house. My grandmother's tea set, sent through the mail wrapped like it was surviving the end of days. This time is the short time before the end of days and I know we've thought that for thirty years but I was nine then and it seemed plausible and now I feel it coming closer and each future-facing moment hits a high note of absurdity. The chaser to follow every funeral, every marriage, every newborn child. Imagine the small boy with abundant blond curls in twenty years, what is his life like. Today he shows me things over the air, says my name, shows me something else. He's drawn his brother and he, a freshly minted two-year-old, carries the blackboard across the room into my line of sight. I can't stop thinking about all the water in the world and all the mouths to drink it. Their laughter rings and rings and rings in the background. There's no good end to this, just this.

This is a love poem

When time started again after it had stopped it felt new again even though at this point it was very old. The stopping and the starting and the starting after stopping are things that have shapes we should know but never do. I can't count. You can't count. Time definitely cannot count it just happens. But the counting also happens under our breaths and without us. I have counted my way through many indignities and back out again. How numbers exist when I don't think about them is one of the things I like best about them. I let you say many words unto me. Words I would never say to myself. Words you would never say unto yourself. But you say them and then they are said. It is a release of sorts. The shape, the shape of the things we don't say to each other. It is the shape of the entire universe. The entire universe is things unsaid and any pact to start saying things out loud is only as good as the actions that follow it up. Or is it only as good as another you and me and how when we hug our necks are pressed together and I can feel your love for me like a real, true, physical thing. In that moment there is almost nothing else except for the deep quiet that is you loving me and me loving you. Not all of the yous and mes reach this point. This you and me won't get there. Not now. We have shifted apart like the edges of the earth, the immense internal pressure of ageing and the associated decay. The names we have and the names we say and the names that have power over us are like layers that rub and shift and form blisters under both soft skin and skin hardened and calloused. The end is very simple for this you and me. I just walk out. The outside is fresh and cold and I look up into the endless opening sky.

Emptied

You had your ribs removed. I can see it in the lack of shape of you. Standing in a room where you are where everyone tells me I'm ageless tho I'm ageing at a rate like half-lives like a blink cuts me in half and all the men I care for in this space come down to my level to tell me I've not changed, never changed. And the Czech one sees inside me to what is a calm centre and he disbelieves it but believes it but shakes himself like a dog through our speech. His shock is sweet and made out of the deep brown of his eyes and the way he pulls me into the fold of his arm. It is all a type of love. A strange type of love. The love of men set free into the night. Men without ribs without the basic etiquette of affection. Men with eyes like the sun. To look into you is to see myself in another life both backwards and forwards like a spinning top changes direction like your head in silhouette like the silent possibility of two people touching. I am no longer in love with a woman. I am no longer in love with myself. But I am here in this night where only men exist. Where you and I ignore each other like the opposing bells of churches on the same block. Where your empty ribs make space for you to suck your own dick. Where I don't watch. Where I am gone before you see me. Where the night is empty. Where the night empties me of you before I even know it. Where I find myself to have been emptied long ago of all you did.

Good girl, good girl

I think so much the thinking becomes the thing. Then it's just thinking upon thinking upon time and travel and space and you know that even though I think all these minutes and all these hours there's nothing that is quite enough to piece together. I'm never certain. I'm never allowed to be certain. I'm never on top of anything enough to know. The space shapes the time and the time shapes the space. And still, I'm waiting for the space to shape me even though every time it does I am still left waiting. You wouldn't know. You have your own shapes that are driven by different times. I see you and realise the flow of your life is different to mine. Sitting in a dark bar on a sunny day to drink wine and come to you in this space where memory only exists as physical objects. I remember you running your tongue across my lower lip like an animal seeking submission. You wanted me to destroy you just not in the way I eventually did. Many people just see the possibility for ruin inside me. It's the calling out of the part of me that was destroyed as a child. The way a cello will sing an A if you sit a tuning fork on it I'm the song singing of wrack and ruin. I would ruin so many more things than I've let myself if I only let myself. I'm still trying to be top of the class, the good girl. And ruin is not the calling of good girls. Good girls sit with their knees touching with their hands in their laps and with their mouths closed. The good girl's mouth is always closed and the sun never sets and the ruin stays inside where it was put in the first place, where it is meant to be.

Previously published works

'Passive-aggressive letter to a john' was first published in *Landfall* 216, 2008, and in *Best New Zealand Poems*, 2008.

'Landslide' was first published in *Turbine / Kapohau*, 2009.

'The Factory' was first published in *JAAM*, 2012.

'This is a creation myth' was first published in *JAAM*, 2013.

'Ohio' was first published in *Shenandoah*, 2013.

'Sigourney Weaver and the Dream Father' was first published in *Hue and Cry*, 2013.

'Sigourney Weaver and I go to bed' was first published in *JAAM*, 2013.

'Sigourney Weaver buys property in Aro Valley' was first published in *JAAM*, 2013.

'Sigourney Weaver and I rent a movie' was first published in *JAAM*, 2013.

'Sigourney Weaver helps me out of some feelings (not pants)' was first published in *Cordite*, 2013.

'Give up' was first published in *Verge*, 2015.

'Hot spit' was first published in *Sweet Mammalian*, 2015.

'I am a man' was first published in *Cordite Poetry Review*, 2018.

'The heel of your palm' was first published in *This Gender Is a Million Things That We Are More Than*, 2019.

'I invite myself inside' was first published in *Landfall* 238, 2019, and in *This Gender Is a Million Things That We Are More Than*, 2019.

Acknowledgements

The most important thank you for any Pākehā writer is to mihi to all mana
whenua of Aotearoa for their generosity in the face of continued acts of non-
consent and disrespect by us, their Treaty partners. I am truly privileged to be
a Treaty partner, to have this place to stand and to receive repeated gifts and
offerings of manaakitanga. These started in my very early years in Ōtautahi
and continue in my life now in Pōneke. There cannot be thanks or koha enough,
only work towards a true and real partnership that lives up to Te Tiriti.

When you've been writing for twenty-five years before you make a first book,
there's a huge list of people to acknowledge. To go back to 1987 and thank
Ms. Thompson and her dangly earrings at Christchurch East School seems a little
intense, but here we are. The earrings were captivating. First and foremost I
have to thank Sam Elworthy for casually asking what I was doing with my writing
one night in a Wellington pub. It was the prompt I needed to transform reluctance
into curiosity. And a huge thank you to all of the AUP team for making this book
a reality. Thank you to everyone I'm going to forget to thank. A human is made
up of so many others.

Over the years I've been published and selected by a bunch of generous editors,
from Helen Rickerby to Derek Motion to Doc Drumheller and Ciáran Fox to James
Brown to Chris Price to Emma Neale. Some of these poems have appeared in *JAAM*,
Turbine | Kapohau, *Cordite Poetry Review*, *Shenandoah*, *Verge*, *Hue and Cry*, *Sweet
Mammalian*, *Landfall*, *This Gender Is a Million Things That We Are More Than* and *Best
New Zealand Poems*. Thank you to all those editors and publications. Thank you to
Tristan Taormino for being the first person to pay me for my writing in *Best Lesbian
Erotica 2002*. Thank you to all the people who read, published and shared my work.
Thank you to Stuart Hoar for encouraging me when I was about to give up and for
also giving me the most useful writing advice I've ever received. Thank you to
Sugar Magnolia Wilson, Morgan Bach, Hannah Mettner, Carolyn DeCarlo, Jackson
Nieuwland, Ya-Wen Ho and Anna Jackson for being a very good writing group.
Thanks again to Sugar Magnolia Wilson for encouraging me constantly. Thank you
to Chris Tse for being a great working companion on difficult but important projects.
Thank you to the readers, to the writers and to the much-maligned extroverts.
Thank you to Helen Lehndorf and Johanna Aitchison for also being an excellent

writing group. Thank you again to Helen Rickerby for our many hours of conversation and your encouragement from the moment I moved to Wellington. Thank you to Jean Sergent who provided dramaturgical-level editorial advice on earlier versions of this book. I am grateful for the explosion of new writers in New Zealand in the last five or six or ten years. I feel so amazed by so many of you. What glorious company.

Thank you to Dougal McNeill for writing about one of my poems in the *Journal of New Zealand Literature* (no. 27, 2009). Also thank you NZQA for using one of my poems as part of an English exam. I very much enjoyed the comments from bewildered teenagers on a blog post they found when desperately googling for answers.

Thank you to all past, present and future lovers and friends. It is through connection with people that I find myself coming back to writing again and again. Without you and the feelings I have about you all, I doubt I'd ever write anything, and I'm sorry I can't thank you all by name. Thank you, Tria Manley, for everything from that candlewick bedspread dress to now. Thank you to Kenese Lautusi, Craig Spence and Sam Minns for being some of the best men, music makers and clowns I am lucky to know. Thank you to Stevie Wilder for everything from our cuddles to our deep discussions to our left-over roast toasties. Thank you to the one and only Jojo Hall for every single thing we've ever done together plus thank you for letting me in on LLP. Thank you most to my beloved companion of sixteen years, Simon Carryer. You and I have grown together, and this book (and possibly I) would not exist without the joy, humour, love, silliness and deep thinking you bring into my life. Thank you for teaching me to enjoy bush walks. Thank you for every breakfast in bed.

Emma Barnes studied at the University of Canterbury and lives in Aro Valley, Wellington. Their poetry has been widely published for more than a decade in journals including *Landfall, Turbine | Kapohau, Cordite* and *Best New Zealand Poems*. They are currently co-editing with Chris Tse an anthology of LGBTQIA+ and takatāpui writing from Aotearoa New Zealand for Auckland University Press.

First published 2021
Reprinted 2023
Auckland University Press
University of Auckland
Private Bag 92019
Auckland 1142
New Zealand
www.aucklanduniversitypress.co.nz

ISBN 978 1 86940 938 8

A catalogue record for this book is available
from the National Library of New Zealand

Epigraph p. 47 credit: Maggie Nelson,
excerpt from *The Argonauts*, pp. 152–53.
Copyright © 2015 by Maggie Nelson.
Reprinted with the permission of
The Permissions Company, LLC on
behalf of Graywolf Press, Minneapolis,
Minnesota, graywolfpress.org

Design by Greg Simpson

Printed by Bluestar, Wellington